About this book

This book is for everyone who is learning their first words in German. By looking at the little pictures, it will be easy to read and remember the German words underneath.

When you look at the German words, you will see that in front of most of them there is **der**, **die** or **das**, which means "the". When you are learning German, it is a good idea to learn the **der**, **die** or **das** which goes with each one. This is because all nouns or naming words, like cup and table, as well as man and woman, are masculine or feminine, and some words, like book and bed, are neuter. **Der** means the word is masculine, **die** means that it is feminine and **das** means that it is neuter. **Die** is also used if the word is plural, that is, there is more than one, such as tables or books. You will also see that all nouns in German begin with a capital letter (big letter).

Some of the words have an a, o or u with two dots above, like this **ä ö ü**. The two dots are called an umlaut, and they change the way you say the a, o or u. There is also a special letter **ß**, called an es-zet, for the ss sound.

At the back of the book is a guide to help you say all the words in the pictures. But there are some sounds in German which are quite different from any sound in English. To say a German word correctly, you really need to hear a German speaker say it first. Listen very carefully and then try to say it that way yourself. But if you say a word as it is written in the guide, a German person will understand you, even if your German accent is not perfect.

Usborne
First hundred words
in German

Heather Amery

Illustrated by Stephen Cartwright

Designed by Mike Olley and Jan McCafferty

Translation and pronunciation guide by
Mairi Mackinnon and Fiona Chandler

 There is a little yellow duck to find in every picture.

Das Wohnzimmer  The living room

Vati
Daddy

Mutti
Mummy

der Junge
boy

das
Mädchen
girl

das Baby
baby

der Hund
dog

die Katze
cat

Die Kleidung Clothes

die Schuhe
shoes

die Unterhose
pants

der Pullover
jumper

4

das Unterhemd
vest

die Hose
trousers

das T-Shirt
T-shirt

die Socken
socks

Das Frühstück Breakfast

das Brot
bread

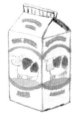

die Milch
milk

die Eier
eggs

6

der Apfel
apple

die Orange
orange

die Banane
banana

Die Küche The kitchen

der Tisch
table

der Stuhl
chair

der Teller
plate

das Messer
knife

die Gabel
fork

der Löffel
spoon

die Tasse
cup

Die Spielsachen Toys

das Pferd
horse

das Schaf
sheep

die Kuh
cow

10

das Huhn
hen

das Schwein
pig

der Zug
train

die Bauklötzchen
bricks

11

Bei Oma und Opa At Granny and Grandpa's house

Oma
Granny

Opa
Grandpa

die Hausschuhe
slippers

12

der Mantel
coat

das Kleid
dress

die Mütze
hat

Der Park The park

der Baum
tree

die Blume
flower

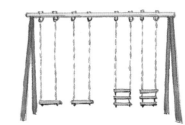

die Schaukeln
swings

der Ball
ball

die Rutschbahn
slide

die Stiefel
boots

der Vogel
bird

das Boot
boat

15

Die Straße The street

das Auto
car

das Fahrrad
bicycle

das Flugzeug
plane

der Lastwagen
truck

der Bus
bus

das Haus
house

Die Party The party

der Ballon
balloon

der Kuchen
cake

die Uhr
clock

das Eis
ice cream

der Fisch
fish

die Kekse
biscuits

die Bonbons
sweets

Das Schwimmbad

The swimming pool

der Arm

arm

die Hand

hand

das Bein

leg

die Füße
feet

die Zehen
toes

der Kopf
head

der Po
bottom

21

Der Umkleideraum The changing room

der Mund
mouth

die Augen
eyes

die Ohren
ears

die Nase

nose

die Haare

hair

der Kamm

comb

die Bürste

brush

23

Das Geschäft   The shop

rot
red

blau
blue

grün
green

24

gelb
yellow

rosa
pink

weiß
white

schwarz
black

Das Badezimmer The bathroom

die Seife
soap

das Handtuch
towel

die Toilette
toilet

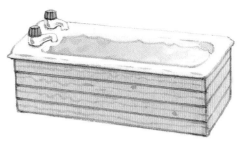

die Badewanne
bath

der Bauch
tummy

die Ente
duck

Das Schlafzimmer The bedroom

das Bett
bed

die Lampe
lamp

das Fenster
window

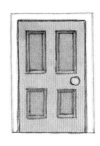

die Tür
door

das Buch
book

die Puppe
doll

der Teddy
teddy

29

Match the words to the pictures

der Apfel

das Auto

der Ball

die Banane

das Buch

das Ei

das Eis

die Ente

das Fenster

der Fisch

die Gabel

der Hund

die Katze

der Kuchen

die Kuh

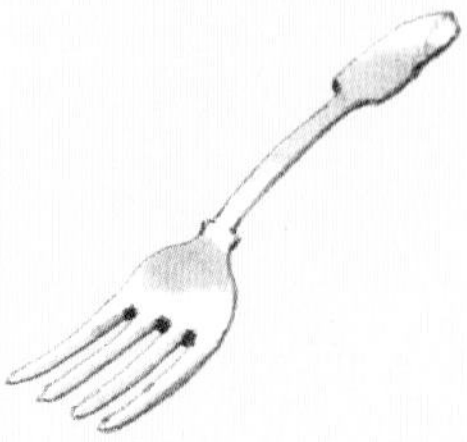

die Lampe

das Messer

die Milch

die Mütze

die Orange

der Pullover

die Puppe

das Schwein

die Socken

die Stiefel

der Teddy

der Tisch

das Unterhemd

die Uhr

der Zug

Die Zahlen   Numbers

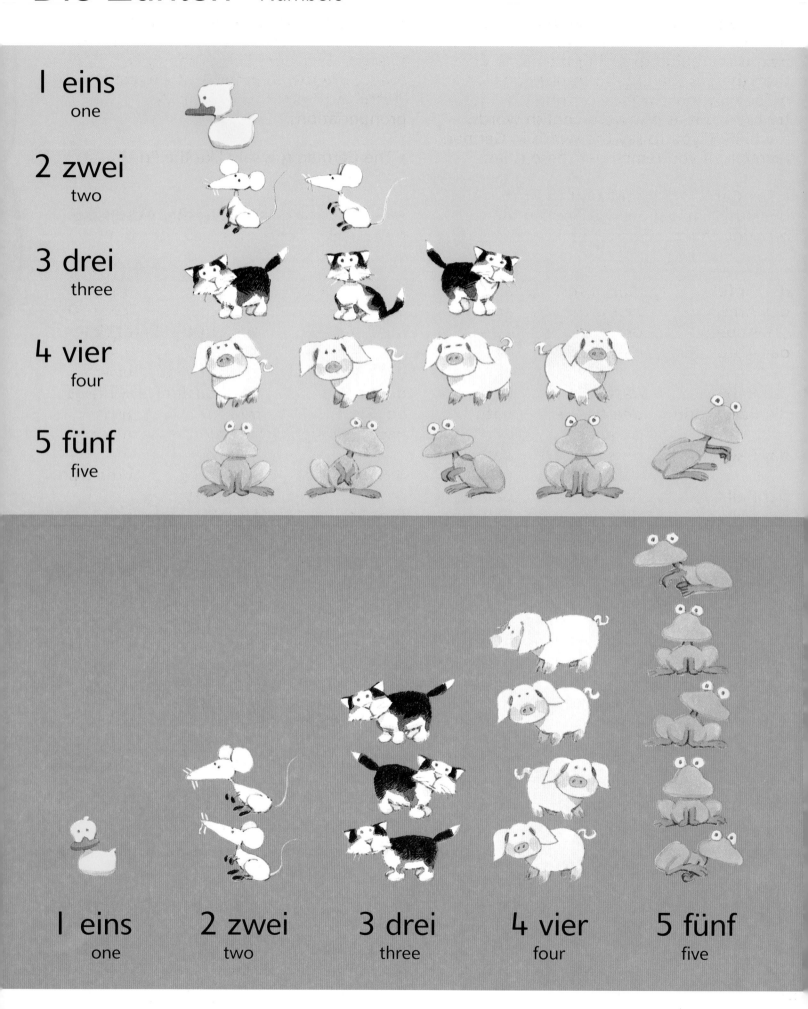

1 eins
one

2 zwei
two

3 drei
three

4 vier
four

5 fünf
five

1 eins
one

2 zwei
two

3 drei
three

4 vier
four

5 fünf
five

32

Words in the pictures

In this alphabetical list of all the words in the pictures, the German word comes first, next is the guide to saying the word, and then there is the English translation. The guide may look strange or funny, but just try to read it as if it were English words. It will help you to say the words in German correctly, if you remember these rules:

• The German **ü** is said a bit like the "u" in "music". It is shown as "ew" in the pronunciations.

• The German **ch** is usually said like the "h" in "huge". After "a", "o", "u" or "au" though, **ch** is more like a grating "h" sound, like the **ch** in the Scottish word "loch". It is shown as "kh" in the pronunciations.

• The German **g** is said like the "g" in "garden".

• The German **r** is made at the back of the throat and sounds a little like growling.

der Apfel	*dair apfel*	apple
der Arm	*dair arm*	arm
die Augen	*dee aowgen*	eyes
das Auto	*dass aowto*	car
das Baby	*dass baby*	baby
die Badewanne	*dee bahder-vanner*	bath
das Badezimmer	*dass bahder-tsimmer*	bathroom
der Ball	*dair bal*	ball
der Ballon	*dair ba-lawn*	balloon
die Banane	*dee banah-ner*	banana
der Bauch	*dair baowkh*	tummy
die Bauklötzchen	*dee baow-klerts-hyen*	bricks
der Baum	*dair baowm*	tree
bei Oma und Opa	*bye oh-ma oond oh-pa*	at Granny and Grandpa's
das Bein	*dass byne*	leg
das Bett	*dass bet*	bed
blau	*blaow*	blue
die Blume	*dee bloomer*	flower
die Bonbons	*dee bon-bons*	sweets
das Boot	*dass bawt*	boat
das Brot	*dass brawt*	bread
das Buch	*dass bookh*	book
die Bürste	*dee bewrster*	brush
der Bus	*dair booss*	bus
drei	*dry*	three
das Ei	*dass eye*	egg
die Eier	*dee eyer*	eggs
eins	*ine-ts*	one
das Eis	*dass ice*	ice cream
die Ente	*dee enter*	duck
das Fahrrad	*dass fahr-rat*	bicycle
das Fenster	*dass fenster*	window
der Fisch	*dair fish*	fish
das Flugzeug	*dass flook-tsoyk*	plane
das Frühstück	*dass frew-shtewk*	breakfast
fünf	*fewnf*	five
die Füße	*dee fewsser*	feet
die Gabel	*dee gah-bel*	fork
gelb	*gelp*	yellow
das Geschäft	*dass gesheft*	shop
grün	*grewn*	green
die Haare	*dee haarer*	hair
die Hand	*dee hant*	hand
das Handtuch	*dass hant-tookh*	towel
das Haus	*dass haowss*	house
die Hausschuhe	*dee haowss-shoo-er*	slippers
die Hose	*dee hawzer*	trousers
das Huhn	*dass hoon*	hen
der Hund	*dair hoont*	dog
der Junge	*dair yoonger*	boy
der Kamm	*dair kam*	comb
die Katze	*dee katzer*	cat
die Kekse	*dee kekser*	biscuits

das Kleid	*dass klyde*	dress	das Schlafzimmer	*dass shlarf-tsimmer*	bedroom
die Kleidung	*dee klydoong*	clothes	die Schuhe	*dee shoo-er*	shoes
der Kopf	*dair kopf*	head	schwarz	*shvarts*	black
der Kuchen	*dair kookhen*	cake	das Schwein	*dass shvyne*	pig
die Küche	*dee kew-hyer*	kitchen	das Schwimmbad	*dass shvim-baht*	swimming pool
die Kuh	*dee koo*	cow			
			die Seife	*dee zyfer*	soap
die Lampe	*dee lamper*	lamp	die Socken	*dee zokken*	socks
der Lastwagen	*dair lasst-vahgen*	truck	die Spielsachen	*dee shpeel-zakhen*	toys
der Löffel	*dair lerfel*	spoon	die Stiefel	*dee shteefel*	boots
			die Straße	*dee strahss-ser*	street
das Mädchen	*dass mayd-hyen*	girl	der Stuhl	*dair shtool*	chair
der Mantel	*dair mantel*	coat	die Tasse	*dee tasser*	cup
das Messer	*dass messer*	knife	der Teddy	*dair teddy*	teddy
die Milch	*dee milkh*	milk	der Teller	*dair teller*	plate
der Mund	*dair moont*	mouth	der Tisch	*dair tish*	table
Mutti	*moottee*	Mummy	die Toilette	*dee twa-letter*	toilet
die Mütze	*dee mewtser*	hat	das T-Shirt	*dass tee-shirt*	T-shirt
			die Tür	*dee tewr*	door
die Nase	*dee nah-zer*	nose			
			die Uhr	*dee oor*	clock
die Ohren	*dee oar-en*	ears	der Umkleideraum	*dair oom-klyder-raowm*	changing room
Oma	*oh-ma*	Granny	das Unterhemd	*dass oonter-hemt*	vest
Opa	*oh-pa*	Grandpa	die Unterhose	*dee oonter-hawser*	pants
die Orange	*dee oran-jer*	orange			
der Park	*dair park*	park	Vati	*fartee*	Daddy
die Party	*dee par-tee*	party	vier	*feer*	four
das Pferd	*dass pfert*	horse	der Vogel	*dair fawgel*	bird
der Po	*dair paw*	bottom			
der Pullover	*dair pull-awver*	jumper	weiß	*vice*	white
die Puppe	*dee poopper*	doll	das Wohnzimmer	*dass vawn-tsimmer*	living room
rosa	*ro-za*	pink	die Zahlen	*dee tsarlen*	numbers
rot	*rawt*	red	die Zehen	*dee tsay-en*	toes
die Rutschbahn	*dee rootsh-barn*	slide	der Zug	*dair tsook*	train
			zwei	*tsvy*	two
das Schaf	*dass sharf*	sheep			
die Schaukeln	*dee shaow-keln*	swings			